The Changing Weather

Grace Waters

ROSEN
COMMON CORE
READERS

Rosen Classroom™

New York

Published in 2013 by The Rosen Publishing Group, Inc.
29 East 21st Street, New York, NY 10010

Copyright © 2013 by The Rosen Publishing Group, Inc.

All rights reserved. No part of this book may be reproduced in any form without permission in writing from the publisher, except by a reviewer.

Book Design: Katelyn Londino

Photo Credits: Cover lafoto/Shutterstock.com; pp. 4, 6 (snow) jonathansloane/Vetta/Getty Images; p. 4 (fall leaves) © iStockphoto.com/Geoarts; pp. 4, 13, 15 (sunny day) leonid_tit/Shutterstock.com; pp. 4, 15 (rain) Jeff Greenberg/Photolibrary/Getty Images; pp. 5, 15 (kids in snow) © iStockphoto.com/skynesher; pp. 7, 15 (kids in park) Derek Latta/Photodisc/Getty Images; pp. 8, 15, 16 (girl with umbrella) Eric Limon/Shutterstock.com; pp. 9, 15, 16 (girl with sunglasses) Sonja Foos/Shutterstock.com; pp. 10, 15, 16 (clear night sky) MarcelClemens/Shutterstock.com; pp. 11, 15 (cloudy night sky) Stanislav Fridkin/Shutterstock.com; pp. 12, 14, 16 (stormy sky) Martin Fischer/Shutterstock.com; p. 14 (sunny field) nadiya_sergey/Shutterstock.com; p. 14 (trees in wind) Paul Aniszewski/Shutterstock.com; p. 14 (snowy trees) Mazzzur/Shutterstock.com.

ISBN: 978-1-4488-8749-1
6-pack ISBN: 978-1-4488-8750-7

Manufactured in the United States of America

CPSIA Compliance Information: Batch #WS12RC: For further information contact Rosen Publishing, New York, New York at 1-800-237-9932.

Word Count: 142

Contents

Weather is what it's like outside.

The weather is always changing!

The weather is cold in the winter. You need to wear a coat and hat to stay warm.

There are many snowy days in the winter.

The weather is hot in the summer.

Kids play at the park when it's hot.

The ground is wet on a rainy day.
You need an umbrella to stay dry.

The ground is dry on a sunny day.
You don't need an umbrella.
You need to wear sunglasses!

We can see stars on a clear night.
There are no clouds.

We can't see stars on a cloudy night. There are too many clouds.

It's loud outside during a storm.
The wind makes a lot of noise!

It's quiet outside on a calm day.
There is no wind.

What kind of weather do you like best?

Weather Opposites

cold

hot

rainy

sunny

wet

dry

clear

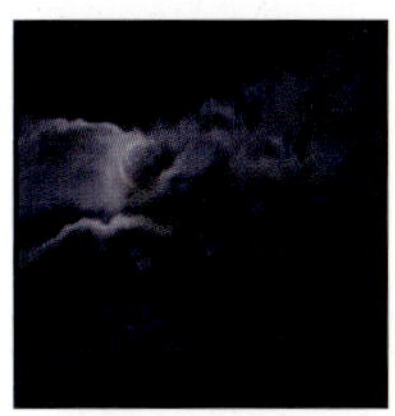

cloudy

Words to Know

clear

storm

sunglasses

umbrella

index